Dance, Gremlin, Dance

A Coming of Age Tale about
Facing Our Fears and Finding Ourselves

By Elizabeth Stallworth Dunwody

Illustrated by Li-An Tsai

Published in 2017 by Regeneration Writers Press, LLC
1177 Adams Street, Macon, GA 31201

regenerationpress.com
editor@regenerationpress.com

ISBN-10: 1-945098-00-7
ISBN-13: 978-1-945098-00-0

Elizabeth Stallworth Dunwody, Author
Li-An Tsai, Illustrator
Margaret Eskew, Publishing Editor
Jerome A. Gratigny, Designer & Technical Editor

Order *Dance, Gremlin, Dance*
from regenerationpress.com
or amazon.com
or Regeneration Writers Press, LLC
1177 Adams Street
Macon, GA 31201-1507

Forward

Dance, Gremlin, Dance is a story excavated from distant childhood memories. It is a tale of divine discovery of our innermost fears and our deepest delights. It is at that breathless intersection that we discover our true selves and are emboldened to confront our fears, finally freeing us to dance, to create, to gasp in wonder at the joy of the heavens and earth, and each precious moment of this priceless life we have been given.

— Elizabeth Stallworth Dunwody

"The privilege of a lifetime is to become truly who you are."

— Carl Jung

Dedication

To anyone who has ever felt compelled to be someone you are not

To Becky & Ravi - midwives to the soul

To Spiritual Directors of all traditions
as you inleash the innate courage and creativity in us all

To my beloved children who were miraculously
born with this wisdom in their hearts

To my husband who has taught me the true meaning of courage

Special Thanks

To Margaret Eskew and Regeneration Writers Press for their
remarkable commitment to empowering writers everywhere and their dedication
"to publishing works that give testimony to the power of writing
to rekindle hopes, dreams, energy, and life itself."

The melancholy child
sat atop the monkey bars
happy-sad, watching
the wind dance
in the leaves of the trees
to the song of the golden finch.

This was her special place,
her very own mountaintop
away from the world,
in which she never seemed to fit.

In the quiet of the late afternoon,
the poems within her
wrote themselves in the clouds,
and her heart sang so beautifully
that the notes emerged from her eyes
and sweetly caressed her checks.

3

As the day began its dying once more,
shadows fell upon the young girl,
silently embracing her –
weaving, weaving the delicate cocoon
from which she would one day emerge
multicolored – to take flight,
fully formed, fully complete,
wholehearted.

As she descended the ladder,
bare feet met the moist blades beneath,
cutting through the daylight dreams,
giving way to an unspoken call...

Come home.

The shadows lengthened
with the setting sun at her back,
moving endlessly towards the elusive
true self before her.

Darkness descended quickly now,
so too her pace quickened.
Fear propelled her as the Presence
drew closer and closer.

She resisted the urge to
run or cry out.
Her feet, now cold,
felt every pebble piercing

her delicate skin.

She rounded the corner
toward home, marked by
the majestic climbing tree,
in which she had perched bird-like
hundreds of times.

Its limbs reached out offering
memories of lazy summer days
of laughter and delight.

The tree held within it
all of eternity,
all of creation,
ever creating through those
who dared to climb into its arms.

13

But the Presence was gaining on her
as if carried by its own wind.

Closer and closer still
it came out of the chill
of the coming night,
its breath now warm upon
the back of her neck.

"Could it climb?" she pondered,
as she considered taking
refuge in the Tree of Life.

She shook her head gently,
attempting to banish this haunting Presence
that pursued her out of her own imagination,
when much to her amazement,
she felt a tentative tap
upon her shoulder.

19

Suddenly she stopped.
Summoning every ounce of courage
in her four-foot something frame,
she drew in a long, deep breath,
preparing to confront
the looming Presence.

She spun around like
a tiny whirling dervish.
Her skirt, full and red,
billowed out, propelling her
with a power all its own.

She barely breathed
now face to face with the gremlin
that only a moment ago had
dared to make its presence known.

21

Time froze in that moment
beneath the Tree of Life
before the mischievous
little imp bowed deeply
with feathered hat in hand.

Extending an outstretched arm
and with a welcoming grin,
the curious voice asked,
"May I have this dance,
my dear?"

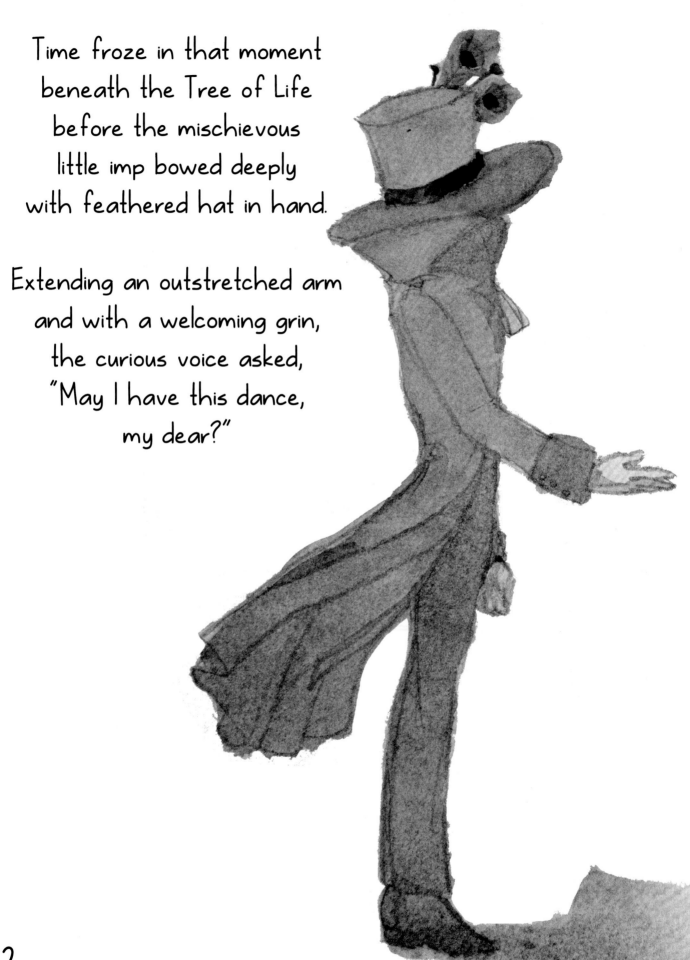

The lonely little girl giggled
as only little girls can and replied
with a regal curtsey,
"It would be my pleasure."

And with that, they danced
the stars into being,
and the old man in the moon
smiled down upon them.

Afterward

This simple parable was birthed deep in the barren majesty of the desert of
Northern New Mexico at a sacred retreat center called Casa del Sol.
It was conceived out of the union of contemplation,
soul searching, and self-awareness.
It is the child of the Great Mystery, and as such,
can never be fully explained.

It is offered as a gift of self-discovery and acceptance that everyone,
of whatever belief, background, nationality, ethnicity,
orientation, and gender identity might hear these words,

"You are my beloved child in whom I am well pleased.
This is how I made you, uniquely you."

Celebrate your authenticity!
Your voice will encourage and empower others
in these turbulent and polarized times.

Welcome to the Dance of the Wholehearted.

Illustrator

Li-An Tsai was born in Taipei, Taiwan and moved to the United States at the age of nine, speaking only her native tongue, Mandarin Chinese. As she learned the English language, her artistic skills enabled her to communicate as she acclimated to what was for her a foreign land.

Her love of art lies in its simplicity, "All I need is paper and a pencil." Soon after her arrival in the states, she discovered the studio sanctuary that is The Creative Alternative, where she honed her innate talent under the tutelage of studio owner, Brooks Dantzler, and instructor, Ray Snyder.

Author

Elizabeth Stallworth Dunwody was born in Georgia but lived in
multiple cities in California, Hawaii, Arizona, and Washington
by the time she was eight years old. She spent her formative years
in the lush environs of the Pacific Northwest.

She possesses the unique ability to relate to people from all walks of life,
having worked as a corporate executive, communications consultant,
and storyline editor and producer on multiple national award-winning projects.

In 2014 she successfully completed the clinical track of
The Daring Way™ national training and certification program.
As a Spiritual Director, she is highly skilled in the ancient art of
sacred listening. In addition to her writing, she continues to consult
with clients from varied traditions and professions.

Selected Books Published by Regeneration Writers Press, LLC

Mr. Tuck and the 13 Heroes by John Harris and illustrated by Sophie Harris. Macon, GA: Regeneration Writers Press 2016. $19.95 (hard cover) A true story of the integration of the first school in Henry County in Georgia, this book narrates for children and adults one of the shining moments from this tumultuous period, recounting how the kindness of the elementary school principal was repaid years later by the actions of the then little girl as he lay half-conscious on a hospital bed. A beautiful story with winsome pictures, this book is a testimony to the goodness that lies sometimes dormant in each of us and can gently guide us, children and adults, as we seek to join the too often polarized conversation on race in American society.

Regeneration! A Journal of Creative Writing 2016. ISBN 978-0-9843747-9-3 Macon, GA: Regeneration Writers Press, 2016. $15.95 (soft cover) You may laugh at the antics of hens and goats, or chipmunks in a mattress. You may be sad watching a family break apart or a little boy miss his mama. You may get angry at the injustice of those who try so hard and still haven't quite gotten there. You may discover something about yourself and the way you may have treated others in the past. The offerings here are not just about reading for entertainment. They are about giving voice to a variety of writers. Get yourself caught up in the energy of first love, the innocence of marriage on death row, the pain of life-altering divorce, the incessant interaction of siblings, fatherhood gone violent, the gentle spirit of a grave-digging preacher, a measured reflection on truth, the musical legacy of a Macon jeweler, and the power of forgiveness in a local prison.

The Reason of Fools by Dodie Cantrell Bickley. ISBN 978-0-9843747-3-1. Macon, GA: Regeneration Writers Press, 2012. $19.95 (soft cover); ISBN 978-0-9843747-5-5 Macon, GA: Regeneration Writers Press, 2012. $24.95 (hard cover). An historical novel set mainly in WWII Germany, the novel interweaves the struggle of non-NAZI Germans during that period with the continuing struggle of African Americans for human rights as they put their lives on the line to achieve victory over the NAZIs. It is also the coming of age story of the author's mother and her love-hate relationship with an American GI from the South. It details the troubled relationship and exploits of the GI and his childhood friend, both sons of Southern preachers, one white and one black. The historical facts have been thoroughly vetted for accuracy. This is a popular book-club selection.

A Reason to Fear by Dodie Cantrell Bickley. ISBN 978-0-9843747-7-9. Macon, GA: Regeneration Writers Press, 2014. $24.95 (hard cover). This historical novel is the second book in The Reason trilogy. It follows the same characters during the early years of the American occupation of Germany following the Allied victory in 1945. The on-again, off-again romance between the American GI and the beautiful young Fräulein stalls until the GI gets orders to return to Germany. He witnesses the dire effects of the Non-Fraternization policy and the toll American ideas about race have exacted from his African American childhood friend and war buddy. Troubled religious beliefs overlie much of the page-turner narrative. This book is used in book clubs, literature and history classes, and in classes that deal with issues of justice.

Gold Stone by David & Donna Lane. ISBN 978-0-9843747-8-6. Macon, GA: Regeneration Writers Press, 2014. $14.95 This is a picture book with a sad, but beautiful story, told by master storytellers for people 8 to 80. Anyone who has ever suffered a loss would benefit from reading this book. It is the narrative centerpiece for a curriculum to deal with Post Traumatic Stress disorder. Motivated by the challenge to develop a program to help Haitian pastors, counselors, and other leaders address the trauma that affected their people after the devastating earthquake, the author dug into history and into the culture of the Haitian people to identify a story that would resonate with their keen sense of loss. Up-and-coming Georgia artist Yvonne Gabriel created the winsome illustrations that mirror the loss of the young prince and his eventual decision to reclaim his life. This book is presently being used to address trauma in at least ten countries. It has been translated into Haitian French.

Chico The Polar Bear by Yvonne Gabriel. ISBN 978-0-9843747-1-7. Macon, GA: Regeneration Writers Press, 2010. $19.95. This is a beautiful picture book about a polar bear who wants to leave the North Pole and sun himself on the beach. When he gets too hot, he shaves off his fur and nearly freezes to death upon his return. His buddies make fun of him because of his loss of hair. He skulks silently away and almost freezes to death before a little girl finds him and saves his life. He eventually reunites with his buddies and forgives them for laughing at him and admits his own culpability. The book has been placed in the rooms of children with cancer. Without being didactic, the story teaches self-acceptance, forgiveness, and admission of personal error—something all of us need to learn.

Regeneration! A Journal of Creative Writing 2010. ISBN 978-0-9843747-0-0 Macon, GA: Regeneration Writers Press, 2010. $15.95 (soft cover) A collection of authentic Southern stories, essays, poems, and interviews, written, selected, and edited by working adult students who found their voices in a writing class. A smorgasbord of short pieces packed with the power of personal experience and sometimes Faulkneresque situations, characters, and experiences delights and invites readers to sample just one more story. Used successfully to motivate other working adult, GED, and international students of English, the book is a testimony to the richness of experience, the seriousness of purpose, and the dedication to achievement that working adults bring to the academy. It has been used to motivate readers in programs in at least four countries.

Light in Dark Places by Duane Davis. ISBN 978-0-9843747-2-4 Macon, GA: Regeneration Writers Press, 2011. $14.95 (soft cover) Motivated by the desire to leave a legacy for his grandchildren and to express appreciation to scores of former students and colleagues, the author, with an honesty that is compelling, pulls back the veil of religion to reveal the books that have most influenced his personal religious journey. In the foreword, ethics writer Dr. Colin Harris describes the book as a "helpful mirror in which to see the better parts of ourselves and . . . as a clear and hopeful lens through which to see the rest of the world." This book has been used in classes in religion and ethics and also by Bible study groups and for personal meditation.

The Cannon Ridge Stories by Robert N. (Bob) Mathis, Sr. In preparation. Poignant coming-of-age-stories from the real life experiences of boys from ten to eighteen working summers on Uncle Joe's farm in North Georgia, where their parents sent them to keep them off the streets of Atlanta and earn money for school clothes.

No Good Reason by Dodie Cantrell-Bickley. In preparation. Vignettes of the Viet Nam war years seen through the eyes of a child chronicle the lives of Bud and Liselotte (*The Reason of Fools* and *A Reason to Fear*) as they navigate American hostilities toward Germans post WWII and increasing civilian anger over American involvement in Viet Nam against the backdrop of the Civil Rights struggle energized by returning black WWII soldiers.

Daybreak. In preparation. Editor Sharon McElhaney and Portrait Artist Yvonne Gabriel. Stories of the Homeless and Marginalized in Macon, Georgia, it includes ten original portraits depicting individuals on the margins, a short history of the founding of Daybreak, and a poignant essay on homelessness by Mercer Chancellor and acclaimed author Dr. R. Kirby Godsey.